NLP

Speed Reading, Subliminal Persuasion, And Mind Control Are Three Of The Most Powerful Dark Techniques That May Be Used To Influence Other People

(Learn The Art Of Person To Person Analysis And Develop Your Persuasive Abilities)

NikolausHofinger

TABLE OF CONTENT

Machiavellianism 1

The Usefulness Of NLP In Educational Settings 7

The Status Of The Rapport 40

Obtain Everyone's Favorite Status 47

Characteristics Of The Dark And An Explanation Of Dark Psychology 55

The Techniques Of Nlp 65

In What Other Contexts Might You Find It Useful To Ask Questions? 72

An In-Depth Explanation Of More Complex Tactics 81

What Daffodils, Psychopaths, And Machiavellians Have In Common With Each Other 92

The Neuro-Linguistic Programming Communication Model 97

How People May Be Manipulated And Influenced In Their Day-To-Day Lives Via The Use Of Psychological Principles 107

Subversive Methods Of Influence 113

Using NLP In Your Everyday Life And Relationships 118

What Are Some Of The Benefits And Drawbacks Of Manipulation? 128

Techniques Often Used In Nlp 143

Workouts That Focus On Building Muscle 167

Machiavellianism

The individual who has Machiavellian personality characteristics does not stop to evaluate if the acts they do are the most efficient way to achieve the objectives they have set for themselves. However, there are other options that do not need lying, treachery, or considering if the consequence of their acts would be worthwhile in the end. The Machiavellian personality is not evidence of a strategic or calculating mind trying to achieve a worthy goal in a contested setting, since this would need strategic thinking and calculation. Instead, everything hinges on whether or not the circumstances need a calculated, cold, and manipulative attitude or not. This question must constantly be asked.

As an example, all of us had phoned in sick to work when what we really wanted was a day off. However, for the vast majority of us, this kind of behavior is not indicative of who we typically are, and after engaging in such dishonest behaviors, many of us experience feelings of remorse. Those who exhibit a high level of Machiavellianism would not only lie in order to get a day off work; rather, they consider dishonesty and lying to be the sole appropriate way to behave oneself in any circumstance, regardless of whether or not doing so yields any advantages. In addition to this, because Machiavellian personalities who successfully attain political power are accorded a certain degree of social acceptance and tacit approval, their presence in society does not receive the same kind of negative attention as is accorded to the other two members of the Dark Triad, namely psychopathy and narcissism. This is because of the degree of social acceptance and tacit approval accorded to Machiavellian personalities who successfully attain political power.

The trait of narcissism

The ancient Greek tale of Narcissus, a young man who saw his reflection in a pool of water and fell in love with the picture of himself, is where the name "narcissism" comes from. In the field of clinical psychology, Sigmund Freud was the first person to describe narcissism as a disease. Since then, narcissism has been consistently included in official diagnosis manuals as a description of a distinct form of mental personality disorder. Narcissism is described as a disorder that is characterized by an inflated feeling of importance, an excessive demand for attention, a lack of empathy, and as a consequence, dysfunctional relationships. This definition comes from the field of psychology.

Outwardly, narcissists may exhibit an excessively high level of confidence; nevertheless, behind this facade is often a highly fragile ego and a great degree of sensitivity to criticism. Narcissists are notoriously difficult to read. There is often a significant gap between a narcissist's very positive perception of oneself or herself, the resultant expectation that others should show him or her favors and special treatment, and the disappointment that follows when the consequences are rather negative or otherwise different from what the narcissist had anticipated.

These issues may manifest in the narcissist's personal life, professional life, and financial life, among other aspects of the narcissist's existence. Those who have characteristics that are indicative of Narcissistic Personality Disorder (NPD) are at risk of engaging in relationships that are characterized by a lack of empathy. This risk is associated with the Dark Triad.

For instance, a narcissist may want frequent remarks, attention, and praise from his or her relationship, yet the narcissist will often look unable or unable to reciprocate by exhibiting care or reacting to their partner's concerns, ideas, and emotions. Narcissists, on the other hand, exhibit a sense of entitlement and anticipate receiving an excessive amount of praise and recognition, even though, in most cases, they have never earned or performed anything that would warrant such emotions of entitlement.

In addition to this, they have a propensity to be too critical of the people in their immediate environment, and they have an exaggerated reaction to any criticism, even the mildest kind, that is leveled at them. As a result of this, the idea of narcissism in popular culture is often employed as an insult and a derogatory word. In a similar manner, this trait is also shown by people who have high levels of love and contentment for themselves.

Having healthy self-esteem is not the same thing as having neurotic personality disorder (NPD), which is a psychiatric term. Understanding that the narcissist's view of oneself or herself is often entirely idealized, grandiose, and inflated and cannot be supported with any true, significant achievements or abilities that may make such claims plausible is the key to comprehending this part of dark psychology. The conduct of a narcissist that is demanding, manipulative, inconsiderate, self-centered, and arrogant may create issues not only for the narcissist's own life but also for the lives of other people because of the dissonance that exists between their expectations and the reality of the situation.

The Usefulness OfNLP In Educational Settings

It is impossible to deny that there is at least a little bit of uncertainty about the efficacy of NLP, despite the fact that we are now familiar with what NLP is, how it operates, and its connection to the enhancement of one's capacity for learning. However, there is no need to be concerned since, as you will see in the passages that follow, there have been in-depth evaluations and research carried out in the past that may either verify or disprove the efficacy of Neuro-Linguistic Programming.

Surprisingly, Natural Language Processing (NLP) has become the focal point of controversy and discussion among the scientific and psychiatric sectors. Tosey and Mathison found that there had not been a sufficient amount of study done on NLP, which they concluded from their examination of the research that had been done. There aren't too many scholarly papers and articles that are circulating about how effective it is and how it's supported by scientific data. In addition, the theoretical foundation of NLP itself has been called into doubt by several academic communities. Due to the lack of an exhaustive and all-encompassing study on NLP, there was only a small amount of research done to find answers to the questions placed on the development of NLP.

There was a recorded poll done on NLP, which goes against the arguments that are forced by those who are not in favor of the model. The poll was conducted in the middle of 1997, and it included responses from 192 people who have completed any level of NLP certification training. According to the findings, the NLP training that the graduates had received was met with an extremely high degree of contentment on the part of the graduates, and nearly no reports of discontentment were found to be present.

In spite of the divergent claims and pieces of evidence on the efficacy of Neuro-Linguistic Programming, it is essential to keep in mind that the findings regarding the question of whether or not NLP is in fact successful may be rather variable. As was discussed before, NLP is a learning approach that requires the participant to engage not just their brain, but also their whole being in order to be successful.

Therefore, the cumulative effort of the learner may be a significant element in determining whether or not he is successful in his profession by making use of the NLP approaches.

I want you to know that ___: "I want you to know that any time we have an issue, I am here to help." The reassurance that the consumer receives from hearing phrases such as "I want you to keep coming back to us for more" After-sale support is a significant factor in determining the number of repeat customers.

___until such a point that___.

When it comes to creating long-lasting relationships with customers, a little amount of encouragement goes a long way. It just takes a few well-placed words, such as "Know the product to the point where it becomes a part of you" or "Keep visiting our store to the point where it becomes your second home!" to firmly plant the concept in the mind of the client.

When you envision picturing yourself as anything else, then you will:

A hypnotic effect is produced if the vendor includes an immediately following operative phrase in their sentence structure. For instance, "When you imagine imagining yourself putting this product to use, then you will realise why you should buy one right away!" This induces mental images in the prospective purchaser, which is important since, as everyone knows, a picture is worth a thousand words.

Why is it necessary to ___.

When a seller asks a customer helpful questions like "For what purpose, may I ask, are you looking at this product?" the buyer is given the impression that the seller has expertise and is capable of providing an educated conclusion. Because customers like having options to choose from, the phrase "I could help you through the various choices we have..." introduced to the sales pitch will naturally pique the buyer's attention.

It's possible that you'll encounter ___, and if you do, that indicates ___.

When selling a product that needs an explanation that is only somewhat detailed and that may or may not appeal to the consumer, you just need to show the product in a different manner. For instance, informing the consumer that "You may experience a little confusion and that means you are getting used to it" would leave them aware and ready for anything may come their way.

Make an effort not to ___.

If you say something like, "Try to resist ordering more after you try this one," or "Try to resist the chance to walk away with a prize," you will be acting in a reverse psychological approach, which will bring you the outcomes you want.

Not only does it make your room fresh, but it also has a light aroma to it: "Not only does it make your room fresh, but it also has a mild fragrance to it!" alternatively, "Not only do you get a discount, but you also get a gift coupon!" The way in which these lines are constructed gives the impression to the consumer that he or she is receiving more value than what they are paying for. This dual feature strategy is particularly successful due to the fact that customers are drawn to the concept of additional value.

Consider [both] of these things. How exactly will it ___.

When you give a scenario to the customer that they may think about or fantasize about, it will make them want to make a buy more than ever before. "Give some thought to this. How would it feel to be able to kick back and relax while this product takes care of everything? " or "Just think about it for a second. How could you possibly pass up this once-in-a-lifetime chance to make this product yours at such an incredible price?

Can [will] you: "Can you tell me what exactly you are worried about so that I can try to solve your queries?" or "Will you be able to specify your concerns?" "Can you tell me what exactly you are worried about so that I can try to solve your queries?" This provides the buyer with the option to connect, while also providing the seller with the possibility to identify answers. It's also feasible to begin a query with "May I interest you in...?" or "Would you like me to...?" as other viable beginnings.

It is recommended that you do the following: "To obtain __, you should __, Which would __, I could __"You should follow the set of instructions that are behind the box in order to obtain the best advantage from it. These instructions will help you get the highest amount of productivity possible. In point of fact, I could give you a demonstration of it...

Following these instructions will make it clear to the purchaser that the product does not need any special training or help in order to be put to use. The value of the product is increased inherently whenever it is made clear to the customer what they should and should not do.

Both the State and Its Behavior

As a means of drawing to a close, I would want to circle back around to the state-behavior relationship that is central to the NLP theoretical framework. The condition of the individual being treated is virtually always intended to be improved. Keep in mind, too, that the belief and values filter is closely connected to the state, which I often refer to as a limbic phenomena. It is time for a shift of state when there is dysfunction or a lack of self-actualization in the system. In point of fact, this is an essential component of NLP. The question that arises is how this takes place.

The NLP Communication Model places an emphasis on the normal flow of events throughout the process. It demonstrates how different perceptions might ultimately lead to different behaviors. On the other hand, change usually takes place as a result of causing the topic to move in the other direction on the model. In this context, what I mean is that almost all NLP interventions work by persuading the subject to change their behavior. This, in turn, causes changes in the subject's physiology, state, and internal representations, and ultimately challenges the subject's filters, which are probably the source of the majority of the subject's problems in the first place.

One more time, for this reason, I stress that the distinction between thinking and belief be made clear. By altering one's physical conduct, which should also involve one's internal cognitive processes, one may bring about a change in state as well as ineffective filtering, which is frequently the root cause of dysfunction and/or the sensation that one's capacities are being exceeded.

Putting on a show

Consider two occurrences that have occurred in your life for the sake of this illustration. You are going to need a piece of paper and something to write with in order to participate in this activity. After you have obtained these things, I would ask that you proceed.

I want you to put two words on your paper that represent the two things that are going to happen in the next paragraphs. The first is one that sticks out in your mind as being one that you had fun with. This might be anything that brought you happiness, such as a moment when you were surprised with something lovely or when you got some other excellent news. The second memory can just be a moment when you were bored or it might bring up a few feelings that are somewhat unsettling. This may be an instance in which you were provided with customer assistance that was less than responsive. It is my recommendation that you write the term describing the incident that was nice on the left side of your paper and the word describing the event that was unpleasant on the right side of your document.

Put your responses to the following questions underneath each word:

When exactly did the incident take place throughout the day?

When did this event take place, and what month was it?

When the incident took place, what kind of weather was there?

What is one factor that contributed to you having the reaction that you have toward the event? To put it another way, which of your core values or beliefs most heavily influenced the formation of your viewpoint, and why?

Next, I want you to strike through the term that describes the favorable outcome, and then rewrite it such that it covers the word that describes the unfavorable outcome. Remove the unfavorable term from the sentence. Imagine that the favorable event takes place at the same time of year, during the same month, and with the same kind of weather that you had previously connected with the unfavorable occurrence. Get both your mind and your body to relax, and then focus on identifying how your feelings have evolved.

Now do this practice once again, but instead of crossing off the good phrase, write the negative word over it. You should make an effort to picture the good occurrence happening at the same time of day, during the same month, and with the same weather conditions as those that you previously connected with the positive phrase. Once again, pay attention to how your feelings shift.

The Clauses Concerning Time

Before, after, in the middle of, and ever since are some examples of time clauses.

The use of time clauses is an effective approach to "assume the close." It is assumed that the members of your audience will make the purchase or carry out the activity that you want them to carry out; there is no doubt that they will make the purchase.

The use of time clauses may be particularly hypnotic because they lead individuals to project themselves into the future, to a moment in time when they have already performed the action that you want them to do.

9.) Once you've purchased my fountain pen, you'll quickly realize how simple it is to use.

Take into account the fact that this phrase assumes your product is simple to use. In addition to this, the inclusion of the time clause "after" presumes that the action "buy" has already been completed. Your audience will find themselves incredibly mesmerized by this since they will imagine themselves in the future having already purchased the thing.

10.) Before you acquire my fountain pen, be absolutely certain that you desire the incredible advantages it offers. It is not suitable for all individuals.

Because you are putting the emphasis on whether or not they desire the benefits of your product at this point, it is assumed that the product offers a wide range of desirable advantages. It is important to note the time clause "before." By informing them it's not for everyone and to make sure they truly want the fantastic advantages before they purchase it, you are not just implicitly but also directly placing them in charge of the situation.

Because your message is verified extremely clearly on the conscious as well as the subconscious level when you employ this wonderful Hypnotic Language Pattern, you should definitely put it to use.

11.) Since you are here reading this, you are probably already aware of the incredible value that this product offers.

Let's dissect this statement and figure out why the time clause "since" is such a good fit for it. They are reading it, therefore what you are about to say must be true. "Since you're reading this," you add, "you're already aware of how much value this product has." Again, it is presumed to be the case, but see what may happen when people have different opinions!

Even if they say to themselves, "no, I'm not already aware of how much value it has," they still presume that the goods has worth, which means that they are really already aware that the thing has value. This is yet another really potent hypnotic loop that you may use!

Words That Are Comparable

Examples of comparable terms include the following: more, less, better, and more affordably

Your use of comparative language in your message functions in a manner that is quite similar to that of a "cause and effect" phrase or a "because" sentence. When we get to those topics a little bit later, you'll notice the parallels.

12.) The length of time someone is on my email list determines the amount of useful information they are exposed to.

This line assumes that there are a significant number of persons subscribed to the email list. It also assumes that they have been there for a significant amount of time, that they trust you, and that they have decided to remain for a significant amount of time as opposed to leaving. All of this is predicated on the assumptions that you are well-known and trustworthy, and that you are, in fact, providing the value that you assert that you are.

13.) The sooner you download your product, the sooner you can start reaping the advantages that have been shown.

This line makes two assumptions: the first is that the people in your audience will download your product, and the second is that your product provides advantages that have been shown. Since it doesn't state how exactly they're demonstrated, the reader is free to substitute whichever reasoning makes the most sense to them.

14.) I'll give you twice as much of your money back if you can locate a cheaper product that offers the same or better value.

The use of "if" implies that what comes after it may or may not be accurate. This casts doubt on the possibility that the reader will locate a cheaper product that offers more value; in fact, it raises the possibility that such a product may not even exist. Take note of the fact that this line makes the assumption that not only is your product inexpensive but that it also provides value.

When you use the phrase "double your money back," you are assuming that the customer has already bought the goods and spent the money. Because of this, the reader is led to imagine themselves in the future, after they have already bought your product and have had the opportunity to evaluate its worth. This has a highly mesmerizing effect.

The Status Of The Rapport

How many of us would want to have more friends and be more memorable to others? To feel more at ease and have greater success while attending events for networking? to have a greater number of satisfying dates? To develop stronger connections with our coworkers and get better acquainted with them, yes.

Through the use of NLP, we have the capacity to strengthen our relationships with others by activating their senses of trust and likability. People have a natural desire to engage with those who have views and points of view that are similar to their own. When we feel like we have something in common with another individual, it's enjoyable. It paves the way for a deeper relationship to be built on since it fosters mutual understanding. It gives rise to an inner voice that says, "You and I aren't that different from each other," which might facilitate the formation of friendships. Finding common ground satisfies a fundamental social need that has been imprinted into us through years of living in tribal communities by making us feel heard and understood. When we look for qualities in other people that we aim to have in ourselves, it brings us closer together.

There is a kind of neuron in the brain called a mirror neuron, and it is present in both humans and other primates. Because of these mirror neurons, we are able to witness the acts of another person and feel as if we are executing those actions ourselves when we do so. These neurons activate when we detect actions that are similar to our own, and they also allow us to replicate new behaviors that we encounter in other persons that we think to have a physical ability level comparable to our own. Because we are evolutionarily predisposed to seek out comparable and repeating actions in others as a method of learning new abilities and establishing trust, it should come as no surprise that our subconscious recognizes mirroring and elicits a reaction of trust when it does so.

When we connect with other people, we have the opportunity to make purposeful use of the trust-building impact that mirroring has. Students who take communications and body language classes are often instructed to adopt the stance of the person with whom they are having a conversation. We're becoming better at using neurolinguistic programming so that we can win the other person's trust. When two individuals are strongly involved with one another, this is something that happens organically as a result of that engagement. As students of NLP, we can also use this to our advantage by making a deliberate effort to do so.

It is easy to use mirroring as a strategy to create rapport and trust. During the next discussion you have, you should start paying attention to the other person's body language, vocabulary, and other nonverbal characteristics. Participate in some modest mirroring of factors such as the other person's posture, speaking rate, and intonation. When the other person sits back in his or her chair and you gradually adjust into a similarly comfortable stance, it demonstrates that you and the other person have something in common. You and the other person are both growing more at ease with the discussion. It goes a long way toward displaying respect and equality when the other person uses formal terminology, and you raise up your level of formality to match their level of formality. These indicators demonstrate that you are interested and attention to the discussion at hand, which encourages the other person to respond with trust and confidence.

In a manner that is analogous to the way in which we may use mirroring to make the most of NLP and establish trust with other people, we can also harness NLP to test for mirroring in order to make the most of our knowledge of how engaged another person is with us. We are able to gauge how much we are able to trust that individual based on the information that has been provided to us in this conversation. Because mirroring is something that happens naturally when someone is fully involved, a show of mirroring from the other party is often a positive indicator that they are present in the discussion and wanting to create a connection with you. This is because mirroring is something that occurs naturally when someone is truly engaged. On the other hand, if someone who understands mirroring takes the effort to mirror you, this might be seen as a sign that there is a real desire to connect with that person.

We are able to carry out simple checks to verify for mirroring. Try anything like making a little change to your posture and watching to see if the other person eventually moves into a stance that is more similar to yours. To get a clearer picture of what the other person is thinking, try gradually picking up the pace of your talk and seeing whether they can keep up. Take it easy and watch to see if they can keep up with you. Increase your rate of speed, and watch to see whether they follow you. Whether or whether they do so will be an indication of how actively involved they are in the discussion, which may help you determine the degree to which you can trust that particular individual.

Mirroring is a simple idea that is straightforward to comprehend and put into practice; nonetheless, it is a very effective method for constructing and analyzing connections. When you have your next interaction, give some thought to where there could be possibilities to use this rapport-building quirk of NLP.

Obtain Everyone's Favorite Status.

Not everyone is on the same level when it comes to becoming everyone's trusted buddy, or even being more efficient when it comes to convincing customers, selling a product, or marketing an idea. This is because not everybody has the same amount of experience. You'd probably observe that various individuals have unique ways of behaving, and some of them even have more alluring appearances than others. It is not because they finished high school at the top of their class or because they are much more attractive than you are. Simply said, they have an influence on the individuals who are in close proximity to them.

The good news is that improving your ability to regulate your body and the rest of your activities may help you improve your communication skills as well as the quality of the interactions you have with other people. That is another goal that may be accomplished with the use of certain NLP approaches. Knowing how these strategies function and applying them to the things you do on a daily basis will offer you leverage. Another piece of positive information is that techniques of NLP for creating rapport and influencing people are routinely taught.

The destruction of barriers through conforming behavior

Both animals and people have a tendency to choose the company of other members of their own species when it comes to matters of trust. You have most likely seen this to be true in the classroom or on the job: the instructors or supervisors who are more likely to show favoritism toward you are those who have the misconception that they are comparable to you in some way. When a dad observes that one of his children has taken after him positively in some way, it is only natural for him to have a favorite among his children.

You will discover that when you are attempting to create rapport, what you are really trying to do is convince the other person that you are thinking in the same way as they are. Technically, this is not what it means to "force someone to look at the world your way," but in practice, this is what it means. This indicates that if you offer him with a certain response to a problem, you are making it seem as if an individual who is extremely like to him has devised a solution. This is the case if you present him with that solution. Therefore, he is more likely to be interested in hearing that response. This indicates that there is some degree of validity to the adage "if you can't beat them, join them."

The following is an example of a popular matching behaviorNLP approach that is used to develop rapport. It implies that when you match the physical and verbal behavior of another person, you are more likely to break down the walls that person likes to establish between himself and another person. This is because matching another person's conduct linguistically and physically increases your chances of doing so. Here is an illustration of that:

Person A walks into an audio shop with the intention of purchasing headphones. Person A tells Person B, who is the salesperson, that he like the way the headphones LOOK when they are displayed on the stand; but, he does not want to purchase the same item since it APPEARS suspicious and he is unsure whether or not the stock still functions properly. Person B, on the other hand, does not have any other items in the stockroom that are comparable to the one being sold, and he is eager to make the transaction. Person B responds, "I will take a LOOK," and then examines the product to see whether it is still operating as intended. When he returns, the client is waiting for him, and he informs the customer that "the headphones APPEAR to be fine to me." The deal is closed with Person B.

With that as an example, you would be able to see that the client pays attention to the environment around him, relying mostly on his visual sense. Even if he is attempting to purchase an accessory that he would use with his ears, this is still the situation! Now, Person B is aware that he has a better chance of closing the deal if he emphasizes the fact that he is on the same page as the other person, which means that they have the same point of view when it comes to evaluating different items.

Interrogators for the police and psychologists are both using the same approach to first build a relationship and trust with a suspect, and then to extract information from them. That indicates that when individuals communicate in the same language, there is a greater possibility that they will get along!

Send forth positive vibes.

Do you ever find yourself wondering why those who are charming won't lose their charm no matter what they do to their appearance? You have most likely come across individuals that are either shorter or heavier than you, yet it seems that they have a greater number of friends than you have. You have met individuals who are missing limbs, yet it seems like they are more physically active than you will ever be in your whole life since they have more athletic pals. Have you ever had feelings of envy?

What these individuals do to other people is this: they make it a point to feel and act unstoppable, and the reason why they know they have a far greater life than everyone else is because they make it a point to feel and act unstoppable. The reason for this is that you are likely to attract other individuals who have characteristics that are comparable to yours. Now, if you believe that you are unattractive, inept, and a major failure, you could start worrying about the kind of individuals that are drawn to you because of your reputation.

Simply transform into the kind of person you want to be, and you'll find it much easier to make new friends and have a good impact on those around you. Instead of being angry at the world, adopt a positive attitude and strive to be the best you can be. People will catch up on what you're doing and start following in your footsteps sooner or later. You are going to be glad that you conducted yourself in that manner. You may not recognize it right now, but you will definitely comprehend that in the future.

Everyone Is Preoccupied with Themselves

When you are first introduced to someone, it is not necessary for you to sell yourself most of the time if you want to establish quick connection with that person. That being the case, if you have in the past experienced anxiety while meeting new people, you should constantly consider the possibility that other people prioritize themselves over you and your needs and concerns. When you put it in perspective like way, you don't need to worry about being self-conscious about being put in the limelight when you need to speak to someone you haven't met before. Make it about them and their accomplishments instead!

When you need to speak to others, you do not need to be concerned that you are being observed, as most of the time, they are thinking about and paying more attention to how they act or how they create an impression on you. Calm down and speak to people the way you would want them to react to you if you want them to be receptive to what you have to say. People are receptive and sensitive to their environments. Make this line of reasoning work to your benefit by first acting in a way that subtly mirrors what they are doing, and then offering them a complement in a way that is also subtly worded. This satisfies their need for validation, and they would quickly eliminate the obstacles that are preventing the dialogue from flowing smoothly for both of you if you did this. If you were to acknowledge the positive qualities that they possess, then they would be more willing to share more information about themselves with you.

Characteristics Of The Dark And An Explanation Of Dark Psychology

Before we begin... What really deserves to be called "true dark psychology" is something that is much, much worse than the topics that we are going to cover in this article. There are various elements to dark psychology, but for the sake of this discussion, we will concentrate on the less dark aspects. In this section, we are going to examine the more everyday applications of this science and see how it is utilized to influence our day-to-day lives. If you are seeking for the purest form of dark psychology, such as necrophilia and serial murders, you will not find such topics on our subject list.

There is only one protection that is really effective when up against pure dark psychology... Put in a call to the FBI.

Having stated that, let us now return to our point of view.

Inherent qualities.

As humans, we all have some characteristics. So, can you tell me about them?

Our qualities are comprised of our attributes. The things that make us who we are are our qualities. They are the identities and the things that bind us to the beliefs, the routines, and the personalities that we have. In every person, place, and object, there are defining characteristics that are referred to as traits. They are the defining characteristics of who we are. It refers to the unique behaviors and perspectives that we have. Some are "normal" by the standards of society, while others are without a doubt deemed weird; they are the quirky natures that are buried deep inside us and are sometimes released out.

Characteristics are the features that set us apart from other people and things. They are not just the mathematics that enable us to understand and solve problems, but also a measuring instrument in our everyday life. They are both the physical and metaphysical traits that we possess.

They are the typical and atypical behaviors that we engage in throughout our lives. Any aspect of a person, from their attitude to their shoe size, may be considered a trait.

Similar to how attributes are used to describe mathematics, traits provide the means by which we may define psychology.

Lack of light.

Is darkness only the absence of light, or is it a blackness as well? It is up to history's most eminent thinkers to resolve this conundrum or dilemma. In the framework of this discussion, we are going to look at darkness from three different perspectives. Both black and white. Moreover, gray.

We may determine how dark or black a thought is by using this chromatic method of looking at light and dark. One may cope with and manage a light manipulation in a very different manner than one would a dark manipulation.

When dealing with psychological issues, the shades of gray that exist between are always a consideration. This is what the study of mental processes entails.

Our thoughts are not limited to either black or white. In point of fact, the brain is made up of graymatter, which are the cells.

Aside from the joking.

The intricacies of our brains cannot be reduced to either the things that lurk in the shadows or the things that are revealed by the light. What one person considers to be dark may not be the same for another. The light that one person sees may not be the same light that another person sees. And the gray area in the middle is just a question of the choices and/or preferences of various people under different circumstances.

When discussing the night, we are going to look at both the risks and the potential rewards. The things that are harmful to us and the reasons for this are going to be referred to as dark. The things that are good for us and make life more enjoyable are going to be referred to as light. And of course, anything that is in the middle is gray.

Given the disclaimer that was just presented, the situation is far more ambiguous than it was before. Having said that, every viewpoint is distinctive. And let's not beat about the bush: we are aware of the times when we are and are not in the dark.

Now that the lights are on, let's have a look at what dark psychology is, and after that, we'll be able to extract certain aspects of it that are applicable to daily life.

Dark psychology, like all other branches of psychology, is concerned with the human mind and the possibilities it has. It would seem that the human intellect has no limits to its capabilities. Some people believe that there won't ever be any limits placed on it. Applying any term at all to dark psychology would thus merely be scraping the surface.

Dark psychology is an essential part of being human. It is something that has had an impact on all of the world's peoples and civilizations. It is a fact about all of us that we are flawed and have a wicked side. It is up to each of us as individuals to acknowledge this and to refrain from acting on the most aberrant sentiments and actions that we experience.

The study of how we see the world around us and how we might manipulate that perception to prey on others is known as "dark psychology." We are persons who thrive on having goals to work for, and when those goals are taken away, we start to take this short route to destructive habits. The study of dark psychology is focused on the idea that genuine evil can never be accomplished, despite the fact that there are certain people who get very near.

A psychopath is a predator who does not feel guilt or shame for their activities. A mindset that is characterized by extremes of both thinking and emotion is characteristic of dark psychology. It is the act of making someone else a victim via the use of mental and physical abuse with no apparent purpose. The pattern of bad behavior.

When it comes to dark psychology, the focus is not on the victim. It details the many levels of inhumanity that have been perpetrated. This is the distinction between someone who is unintentionally deluded and a psychopath who is dislocated.

A fundamental presumption of dark psychology is that every one of us is capable of these things. Every one of us sometimes entertains violent ideas. In addition to this, it investigates the external factors that might have an effect on one's capacity to convert thoughts into actions. It investigates both the predator who acts irrationally and those who do act rationally. This new scientific research casts a different perspective on the predicted prey that was traditionally employed by humans in hunting. We have introduced a perverted version of the hunting mindset into our daily lives. It has not been discovered that any other species have the ability to do harm to another individual or entity for no apparent reason. It is strictly a human trait.

Knowledge, according to the calculations of dark psychology, which begins with the premise that every individual has the capacity for evil inside them, may lower the likelihood of anything bad occurring. When we look at the past and the present through the lens of dark psychology, we are contemplating how we managed to make it through the day.

There is a dark continuum that is beginning to assist in the formulation of solutions to the questions of why we behave in the ways that we do. Let's take a peek at a few of the characters' psyches to get a better understanding of the dark continuum.

The disease of narcissism.

A narcissist is someone who is too concerned with themselves. In their minds, it is a given that the center of the universe revolves exclusively about them, and no one else at all. Even love is a weapon in the hands of a narcissist who knows how to wield it. Love for oneself is all-encompassing and complete. It is them loving themselves, and in that blissful state of unconditional love, everything they have ever done is forgiven.

They are the folks that admire themselves the most. The mirror is an object that inspires wonder and reverence rather than anxiety and revulsion. The appreciation causes a continuous transformation in look and character, all of which are concentrated on the individual. When someone is narcissistic, it comes naturally for them to appreciate themselves above all other things.

The narcissist's inflated sense of self-importance no longer allows him or her to be humble. The id of creation and personal embracing, which surpasses all possibility of caring about anything or anyone else, is not something to be proud of; rather, it is a simple reality.

The Techniques OfNlp

Separation from one another

The first item that we are going to look at is a process that is known as dissociation. This is going to be our first topic of discussion. Have you ever been in a scenario when you simply got a very awful feeling about it from the very beginning? If so, describe the circumstances. Or maybe there are certain circumstances that, beyond a certain point, will cause you to feel depressed or down each time you are in that setting. Or, you could have certain scenarios at work that are going to make you quite uneasy, such as a situation where you need to speak in public. In this case, you should prepare yourself for the anxiety that these events are going to cause.

These circumstances will demonstrate the whole gamut of feelings that you are capable of experiencing, and most of the time, they will seem to be things that you are obligated to deal with, as well as ones that are automatic and unavoidable. You will discover, however, that by making use of the strategies from dark NLP and by engaging in dissociation, you will be able to push these sensations out of your mind and stop letting them bother you in the future.

Altering How We View the Content

If you are feeling sad or powerless about a situation, you should use this strategy. The process of re-framing may turn any negative experience into a source of motivation for you by encouraging you to adopt a positive stance toward the meaning of the occurrence.

Let's start with the assumption that you ended a romantic relationship. Let's reframe that, since at first blush it may not seem very appealing. What do it appears like the benefits of being a single person are? To begin, you are now eligible to participate in some future collaboration opportunities. You are free to engage in whatever activities you want, whenever you so choose. And as a result of this connection, you have vital learning under your belt that will help you to have far healthier relationships in the years to come.

All of these are examples of recasting a scenario in a different light. By rethinking the circumstances surrounding the split, you give yourself the opportunity to get a fresh perspective on the situation.

It is natural to experience concern or to linger on fear in anticipated scenarios;

nevertheless, doing so just adds fuel to the fire and causes additional problems. In contrast, shifting your focus to the method you have just described enables you to clear your head and make decisions that are logical and fair to all parties involved.

Anchoring Yourself Ivan Pavlov, a Russian psychologist, is credited with developing the centering technique. Pavlov did his experiments with dogs by continually ringing a bell as the dogs' meal. After ringing the bell quite a few times, he discovered that he can make the animals salivate at any moment just by ringing the bell, even if there is no meat in the room.

It resulted in the formation of a brain link between the bell and the activities of salivating, which is referred to as a programmed reaction.

You should make use of a wide variety of "anchors" in your own stimulus-response work!

When you anchor yourself, you give yourself the ability to attach the hopeful emotional response you want to a specific phrase or experience. You may engage this anchor whenever you feel weak by picking a positive feeling or picture and then intentionally linking it to a particular activity. When you do this, you will be able to activate this anchor, and then your emotions will change naturally.

Recognize what you anticipate experiencing (for starters, self-assurance, pleasure, and calmness, etc.) as a result of your efforts.

Determine where on your body you would want this anchor to be, for example, by grasping your earlobe, massaging your thumb, or squeezing one of your fingertip's.

Consider a time in the past when you were aware of the quality (for example, self-assurance) being discussed here.

While you are recalling the memory, pull, touch, or push the portion of the body that you have selected. You will notice an increase in the feeling whenever you relive the memory. When the relationship state begins to improve, it is time to let off on the strain and keep on deteriorating.

This will build a stimulus-response neurology that, if the touch is rendered again, will activate the condition. To feel the state (for example, esteem), you must make touch with yourself once again in the same way.

Think of another encounter in which you felt the condition, looked through and revisited it with your eyes, and held the condition in the same spot as previously in order to make the response even more positive. The anchor becomes more powerful every time you bring another memory to mind, which will result in a more significant emotion being triggered.

By using this technique, you are able to alter your frame of mind whenever you see fit.

In What Other Contexts Might You Find It Useful To Ask Questions?

When you are speaking to an audience, asking questions that are designed to convince may be beneficial in addition to being useful in management, sales, and interpersonal relationships.

On the other hand, it is highly recommended that you practice your questions in advance of addressing a group of people. Make sure that your questions are catered to the people who will be answering them.

Parents have the power to influence their children's decisions by asking them questions such as the following: "Okay, let's say that you left school for this job. Would you be able to take time off work to go to Europe as you had originally intended during the summer of the following year?

The following is an example of how educators might utilize questions to influence their students' decisions: "You need to enter the science contest." Wouldn't it be great if you won the reward of ten thousand dollars and a vacation to Washington, DC?

The following is a list of frequently asked questions and answers pertaining to the following:

The art of persuasion lies in the use of questions. If you put in a lot of work, you will eventually be able to master it. Before you can learn the skill of asking questions, you will first need to get all of your questions answered. These are the responses to a few of the most often asked questions about the practice of asking questions.

The first question is why it is effective to ask inquiries.

The first reason why asking questions is effective is because it allows the person being questioned to take responsibility of their response. When someone responds to a question, they are showing that they trust the response they gave. They are under the impression that it was their inspiration, and as a result, they find it more persuasive when you make a decision after responding to a question.

Can there be consequences for asking the incorrect questions?

Answer 2: It's possible, but only if your assumptions are incorrect or if they don't match up with your topic.

When I am in the process of asking questions, what additional considerations must I to bear in mind?

Answer 3: Avoid asking questions that might potentially lead to an argument. Instead, you should ask questions that your subject is most likely to agree with, or questions for which you already know the most probable response that they will give you.

A part of society

Your social life is another aspect of your life that may be improved with the help of NLP. This is the method.

The power of networking

Your life will improve in direct proportion to the amount of networking you do. You must not restrict yourself to the circle of persons you are already familiar with. You have to put up the effort to meet people and acquire as many new friends as you can. It's impossible to predict which of them will wind up being the perfect new addition to your group of friends and the one who enables you to get the most out of your existence. You won't only be able to meet new friends, but you'll also be able to keep the ones you currently have.

The obligation to one's community

You will be able to boost your social duty with the aid of NLP. You are aware that it is essential for you to make a contribution to the society in which you live. You are free to donate in any method that strikes your fancy so long as you believe it will assist you in making an effect for the better. Hosting health camps or planning a day full of fun and activities for youngsters are just two examples of what you may do. You will have the opportunity to arrange anything on a massive scale, which will strengthen your ability to take on large-scale tasks in the future.

To reiterate, this is not restricted to only these advantages. As you continue to study NLP, you will become familiar with its myriad of further applications.

The Bonus Ending

The one who doesn't fit. You will, on occasion, come across a potential customer who seems to be interested in purchasing your goods. Although it may seem as if they are interested and give off the impression that they are interested, they will continue to raise objections to all that you have to say. When something like this happens, you have to choose a strategy that is completely against common sense. You have an obligation to let that prospect know that you are unable to assist them and that they should seek assistance from another organization. There are occasions when I even go so far as to tell someone, "We're just not the right company for you."

When I would get clients like this, it used to give my supervisors the willies and when I would go this close to them, it would terrify them to death. They believed that I was trying to avoid making the deal. It does not operate perfectly and requires a certain degree of sensory acuity on the part of the user. The key is to determine how far you can push the consumer away and then wait for him to come back to you on his own. In passing, I might mention that this strategy generates a significant level of trust. When one of these potential customers realizes that you genuinely care about them enough to suggest someone else, they will almost certainly willingly pay extra to you. This is because they feel that you care about them more than anybody else. These individuals value honesty, and one of the ways in which they evaluate it is by maintaining a certain distance from you. When you turn the tables on them and swing the tide in your favor, they will quickly switch roles and begin to pursue you.

An In-Depth Explanation Of More Complex Tactics

We would like to take this opportunity to welcome you to the Advanced Edition of the NLP Sales Course. The purpose of the Advanced NLP Sales Course is to get you to the next level of persuasion that you are capable of. Although this course, in addition to the NLP Sales Course, is based on the most successful salespeople now working in the industry, the advanced course delves much further into the unconscious activation of your client's wants and feelings. Anchoring and a more sophisticated kind of reframing known as Sleight of Mouth are both topics that are going to be covered in this class. These two methods are both far more sophisticated than others like them. However, as long as you give yourself the opportunity to practice each of the procedures in the sequence that I will advise, you will have no trouble putting them to use. By doing the workbook, listening to the audios, and reading the master manual, you can ensure that you have a comprehensive understanding of the original NLP Sales Course.

As a result of teaching these strategies to salespeople, I have seen that one of three outcomes is likely to occur. First, there is the individual who enjoys the knowledge both for its entertainment value and its scholarly interest. The second kind of individual is the one that examines the material and then randomly uses a variety of strategies. And last, there is the individual who has a profound comprehension of the idea of education.

I think the best saying I've ever heard regarding learning is "You've only learned something once you change your behavior." I'm sorry to say that I can't tell you who first spoke those words or who first said them. To this day, I am grateful to whomever bestowed upon me the gift of being able to cite that person. I will be the first to say that throughout my life, I have always been known as the man who likes to "learn." I was always reading and picking up books on the most recent sales and persuasive tactics, as well as the most recent and most cutting-edge information on everything that interested me. "Learning" something only for the sake of amusement. This model has no major flaws that should be taken into consideration. Watching television or participating in other activities that may be considered unhealthy, in my opinion, is not nearly as beneficial as gaining knowledge for the sake of amusement. In this scenario, and for this activity, I do not recommend doing so.

I've also been the person who scans through a book, highlights the "interesting" approaches, and then throws them into practice without any thought or planning. This method does provide the desired outcomes. The issue is that the required number of results are not being produced nearly often enough. Belief is where this phenomena gets its start. You will never be able to cultivate that unshakeable conviction if you do not totally immerse yourself in the system and give up all control to it. That fundamental conviction that these strategies are effective and that you are able to use them successfully.

The third strategy is the one that I think would work best for this specific class. The strategy in which you provide yourself permission to completely alter your actions. ALL effective persuaders are using these new strategies to increase their influence. The fact that you have invested in this training and are making the effort to go through the more advanced content demonstrates, not only to me but also to your subconscious mind, that you are prepared to adopt new beliefs and achieve new levels of success. This means that when you follow the instructions provided in the course, you will instantly have the ability to put what you have learned into practice since the course is intended to educate both your conscious and unconscious minds at the same time. Keep in mind that the only way you will really learn anything is if you alter the habits you now engage in.

NLP and interpersonal connections

One of the primary focuses of our life is on the relationships that we have. We, as human beings, have a deep need to feel connected to one another. We look for it, we experiment with it with love partners, we plan it out with professional colleagues, and we learn how to maintain connections with our family and friends over the course of extended periods of time. There will always be ups and downs in our relationships because we are human beings and will experience them in our own lives as we mature, learn, and take on new experiences. This is why there will always be conflict in our relationships.

Communication is the aspect of relationships that, more often than not, is neglected completely without being examined. When things go wrong, it's possible that it's because we reacted rather than communicating about what was going on. When things are tight and laden with discomfort, it's because communication—specifically, effective communication—isn't a part of the relationship. You are free to speak with anybody in any manner that strikes your fancy. The manner in which you communicate with everyone in your life will be shaped by the beliefs, attitudes, and actions you hold. If you have a habit of communicating through a lens of stress, worry, a lack of trust, and emotions of worthlessness, then the same negative outcomes will occur in your relationship. Your relationship will constantly seem injured, wounded, and uncomfortable if you talk with an aggressive tone and shout names or bully other people.

Language study (sometimes known as linguistics) is a component of learning and modeling in NLP. The manner in which we act and the method in which we understand the world, including how we communicate and how we express ourselves verbally, all contribute to the formation of our overall experience. You will not only learn how to communicate more successfully with your spouse or business partners by using these tactics; you will also learn how to interact more effectively with everyone else.

It Affects Not Only Your Mind but Also Your Whole Body

As soon as you picked up this book, you quickly picked up on the fact that NLP stands for neuro-linguistic programming. It may be translated as the study of the process of human cognition, or the manner in which the brain manifests itself in life and fashions your experience. The mentality is the most important factor. The question now is, what about the body? Your whole physiology is connected to NLP, which not only improves your mental state and your ability to modify your thinking patterns and habits, but also benefits your overall mental health. The brain is responsible for communicating its will to the rest of the body, both consciously and involuntarily. It seems to reason that the procedures in question might be beneficial for more than simply your feelings and your mental capabilities. As a consequence of engaging in NLP practices, significant changes occurred in the body.

The field of NLP places a strong emphasis on language as a means of facilitating the learning of our mental processes; yet, our bodies utilize language just as effectively to interact with ourselves, with one another, and with our experiences. The term for this is body language. How we hold ourselves, how we gesture, where our eyes gaze while we are thinking, remembering, or talking, how we sit or stand, or where our arms are when we approach someone new to make their acquaintance are all examples of ways in which our body language contributes to our ability to communicate. NLP enables one to identify the process that lies underlying all of the ways in which we communicate with our body. One of the approaches that you may utilize in NLP to improve your connections with other people and your body language is called building rapport. You may acquire new skills that will allow you to be open to new experiences, make others feel at ease, and have confidence in all aspects of your life. In addition to your body language, there is also the factor of your current physical health to consider. The degree to which we are aware of how our bodies feel, both positively and negatively, is a significant portion of our consciousness. Do you like to be achy and stiff, or flexible and nimble? Should I be proud of my physique, or should I be embarrassed of it? How healthy or how unwell do I feel?

The issue of our health, both mental and physical, is a source of anxiety for a good many of us. Reframing your habits around self-care, food, and exercise, as well as your capacity to cure yourself, is made easier when you make use of the tools that are supplied by NLP. This training is not going to teach you how to lose weight and stick to your diet;

rather, it is going to teach you how to alter the patterns in your life that prevent you from achieving your objectives. The ideas that will be covered in this training will provide you the skills to learn how to make these changes.

What Daffodils, Psychopaths, And Machiavellians Have In Common With Each Other

These individuals are united in their contempt for other people and in their devaluation of those around them. There are a variety of ways in which each characteristic might be represented. For instance, in narcissism, other individuals are not valued because the narcissist believes that they are the most important person in the world and that they are also magnificent and attractive. Other people are not valued under Machiavellianism since they are seen as nothing more than a means to the end of solving one's own personal difficulties. An incapacity to connect with the feelings of other people might help explain why psychopaths devalue other people. In the minds of psychopaths, other people are similar to lifeless toys.

Other psychological traits, such as ill will, dispositions to lie, and emotional coldness, have been shown to overlap in research at the level of correlations; however, it is not yet feasible to determine which trait is the source and which trait is the result of these connections.

The presence of all three of the characteristics that make up the dark triad together creates a threat to society in the sense that the intrinsic devaluation that is present in narcissism, Machiavellianism, and psychopathy is incompatible with the concepts of equality, the worth of human life, and other principles of social organization. This makes the dark triad a particularly dangerous personality trait. However, other than isolating persons whose cases of these features have reached a critical severity level, it is not yet understood what to do.

Additionally, there is a conceptual connection between narcissism, psychopathy, and Machiavellism. Academic psychologists are working on developing a model that can accurately represent all personality characteristics. When it comes to good characteristics, there is a model known as the big five; but, when it comes to negative characteristics, there was no model for a very long period. In modern times, this function is fulfilled by the dark triad.

Where the Line Between Pathology and Normative Behavior Breaks

The characteristics of the dark triad may manifest in less severe forms of psychopathy, Machiavellianism, and narcissism, but they will nonetheless have an impact on the individual's quality of life and the way he interacts with the world around him.

Experts do not refer to personality disorders when discussing the symptoms of the dark triad since these qualities are within the norm. It is vital to treat these circumstances, but it is not required to isolate the individual since it is most probable that he does not pose a threat to others. A person's level of social integration is one factor that may be used to help determine where the line should be drawn. A person is considered to be within the norm if they do not commit crimes and do not represent a threat to others, yet they nevertheless have characteristics that are typical of one kind.

A questionnaire known as the "Dirty Dozen" (sometimes known as the "dark dozen") is used by psychologists to determine the degree to which narcissism, Machiavellianism, and psychopathy are manifested in individuals in comparison to the average. It is comprised of a dozen questions that enable you to develop unique profiles of the intensity of these characteristics in the responder and answer questions regarding the link with other manifestations, such as decision-making or conduct while in conflict.

Due to the fact that the questionnaire contains a number of inaccuracies, the individual's personal profile does not accurately represent the respondent's characteristics. However, this is consistent across all methods of measurement. Using the intensity of these characteristics, you are able to evaluate the individual differences that exist between persons using the dirty dozen. Because of this, we are in a position to discuss the impact of psychopathy, Machiavellianism, and narcissism on many aspects of human existence and to deal with this information.

The Neuro-Linguistic Programming Communication Model

According to this paradigm, every single person is perpetually caught up in some kind of cycle of their conduct. In addition, an internal reaction is produced as a result of their routine exterior behavior. The individual will then behave in a certain manner as a direct result of the internal response. It is often assumed that a habit created on the outside may also cause a reaction on the inside. As was said earlier, many people feel that the NLP system as a whole suggests that all the external habits are generally created by experiences involving the sensory system. This belief is supported by the fact that the NLP system is rather extensive. This encompasses not just the olfactory and gustatory senses, but also the tactile, auditory, and visual ones.

This indicates that any internal reaction is always generated by the senses, and that these responses in turn cause actions to be shown in a certain manner. Any internal reaction that is generated by any external habit is about a combination of internal processes and the status of the individual's internal environment. And these are the many methods in which one might communicate their sensory experiences. An internal process might be thought of as things like self-talk, a mental monologue, or noises that are generated inside of one's head. Also referred to as an internal state are the experiences, the expressions of one's emotions, and the feelings.

The Most Frequently Employed NLP Strategies

NLP is constantly concerned with tactics; it includes both internal and external habits, and it employs planned methods of both the habits and the reactions. To describe human behavior and the manner in which it might change, it makes use of a variety of different methods and techniques. The majority of the NLP tactics and methods employed are designed to only be used for a limited amount of time. There are recognized tactics that are used, and the manner in which they are utilized frequently and always relies on the application.

Making models

It is generally accepted that modeling served as the inspiration for the idea that would later become known as NLP. The physiology is one method that may be used to determine what a person believes in, and this method is known as the manner. Additionally, it entails having a knowledge of the conceptual plans and methods that individuals use. And in the long term, it has an effect on the conduct of other people, including how they think and how they act in general. In most cases, it is used in order to discover the methods that are utilized and the conduct of the person who is psychologically impacting them, as well as to comprehend the patterns that have been adopted and what is employed in order to fulfill the roles and responsibilities that have been given. For instance, this is when a person learns a new ability or maybe even a language. Another example is when they become fluent in a musical instrument.

When a person is interested in learning a new language, there are three elements in the model that they need to be aware of:

They will need to be familiar with the jargon that is being used as well as comprehend the vocabulary.

The second step is to get familiar with and educate yourself on the syntax. At this point, one is able to piece together all of the individual words in order to form a phrase.

The final model consists of comprehending either the movement of the lips or the movement of the mouth. This is due to the fact that the mouth moves differently in each language, as well as the fact that each language has its own unique pronunciation. And what he gets is the ability to comprehend it and communicate effectively.

According to this view, the models are present in all kinds of routines and routine behaviors. When you have a thorough understanding of each and every pattern of behavior in each of the models, the likelihood of change increases significantly. Take, for instance, the scenario in which you are working and find that the pace at which you answer to emails is unacceptable to you. Or, if you find that it does not meet your expectations, it is time to investigate the model that was used while replying. Make the necessary adjustments to the aspects that you do not like, and hunt for an alternative that is both useful and attractive.

Another method of putting physiology to use is for the controller to instruct the subject in what to do and how to stand or sit. The purpose of rituals, meditation, and breathing exercises is to subtly influence a subject's physiology in order to facilitate the achievement of a desired objective.

A controller may urge a subject to alter their posture or actions in order to make a point by just asking, "Can I show you something about how your body effects your mind?" Once the subject agrees, the controller can then demonstrate the point.

It is common practice for public speakers and seminar leaders to make sure the audience is under their control by asking them to make certain simple adjustments to their posture as a group. For example, they may ask the audience to sit up straight, breathe as if they are very excited, and sit on the edge of their seats (literally) as if the information they are about to hear is the most important information they ever hear. This is done to ensure that the audience is under their control.

Posture, breathing, eye movement, and activity are the primary aspects of one's physiology that may be influenced by conscious decision. A shift in feelings is thus possible via the operation of any number or combination of these factors.

Physical Activity and Physiology

Keep an eye on your disposition and emotional condition. Determine the state of mind you want to be in, and then alter both your posture and your physiology to reflect that state of mind. This can include sitting up straight, jutting your chin slightly forward, and staring upward. Try several variations of smiling just a little bit at different times.

Physiology activity II Suggest to a close buddy that the two of you do an activity together. To get things started, you may ask them, "Can I show you something about how your body affects your mind?" and then see how many different emotional states you can guide them through. Begin with opposing feelings such as melancholy and pleasure, rage and acceptance, fear and exhilaration, hatred and joy, and repulsion and attraction.

while you do this, you want to make sure that the happy feelings are evoked while they are looking at you, and that the negative emotions are evoked when they are NOT looking at you or when they have their eyes closed. This will create a connection between positive sensations and you.

Exercise III in Physiology Create a ritual or activity that gives the person a cause to adjust their breathing, eye movement, posture, and activity level. It may also consist of dancing, drumming, or physical activity.

How People May Be Manipulated And Influenced In Their Day-To-Day Lives Via The Use Of Psychological Principles

People make use of psychology in their daily lives; hence, there is no reason why you cannot make use of Dark Psychology and the strategies it offers to safeguard yourself in your daily life. If you let yourself get consumed by any one of these personality qualities, the consequences might be quite negative. Those who practice sadism are included in this group. For instance, people with this personality type take pleasure in causing pain and anguish to other people, particularly to those who are blameless. They are willing to do this even if it puts them in danger. Those who have the diagnosis of being a sadist believe that inflicting pain on others gives them a sense of pleasure, that it is thrilling, and that it may even be sexually arousing.

It is necessary for us to come to terms with the reality that we often manipulate and mislead other people. When it comes to lying, individuals not only lie to others on a daily basis, but they also lie to themselves on a regular basis. People often lie for the purpose of gaining something or avoiding something. They could do this because they don't want to face the consequences of an activity or because they want to accomplish something and need to fool themselves to do so.

People may fool themselves in a number of different ways, including the following:

Having trouble concentrating on your studies: This kind of thing happens rather often. People who want to study but are easily distracted by a variety of things, notably their mobile devices and the software they use for social media, are a good example of this phenomenon. They are also able to locate almost anything that will divert their attention away from the work at hand. People who are like this seem to have a fear of studying for an adequate amount of time or sufficiently well because they are terrified that if they do so, they will bring home a poor grade, which would demonstrate how stupid they are. Therefore, they engage in the practice of self-deception and devise a notion that would assist them in avoiding engaging in academic pursuits. Should students wind up receiving a poor score on their exam, they will give more credence to this justification in their thoughts. If a person's subconscious is communicating with them, it is advising them that it is in their best interest to have poor marks as a result of their failure to study rather than to study hard and then fail and be seen as being stupid as a result of their performance. They have no choice except to find another solution.

The following is a list of some common ways in which we delude ourselves:

People often lose time by procrastinating whenever they do not like to study or do an activity that is significant. On the other hand, the primary motivation for putting things off can be a fear of falling short of expectations, and putting things off might merely be an excuse. Having confidence in oneself may sometimes be a challenge.

Drinking, using illegal drugs, and engaging in other destructive behaviors - People often engage in destructive behaviors like drinking or using drugs so that they will have someone to blame if they are unsuccessful more than once. This kind of individual will make an effort to persuade themselves that if they could only give up using drugs, they would be able to achieve a great deal of success. despite the fact that they are the ones who are lying to themselves and getting in their own way.

People often keep things to themselves because life is not fair. They have convinced themselves that the world we all inhabit in is an elaborate hoax that the vast majority of people believe in, except for them. It is far simpler to complain that life is unfair than it is for one to accept personal responsibility for not achieving their objectives.

If you have come to the conclusion that you have been fooling yourself, the following are some things that you may take to correct the situation.

Keep in mind that you are quite intelligent, and the fact that you have been able to trick yourself in the past is evidence of this fact. If you were not clever, there is no way that you would have been able to come up with some of those ideas. There is just no way that you could have done so.

It is essential to acquire the skills necessary to conquer your phobias. You have to keep telling yourself that you are more powerful than this and that you can prevail over it, especially if you are trying to avoid a certain traumatic experience or you do not want to take a test.

Last but not least, overcoming your phobias will boost both your self-confidence and your bravery.

Subversive Methods Of Influence

It is often done for the purpose of furthering one's personal interests. According to Immanuel Kant, the only moral method that we may even attempt to affect other people or the conduct that they exhibit is via the use of logical reasoning. He makes it clear that anything else is not just unethical but also immoral as well. How, given this scenario, is it possible for any method of persuasion to be anything other than rational? If we are presented with several options, how is it possible for any aspect of persuasion to be deceptive?

A dark persuader does not operate in this manner at all. They have a distinct purpose in mind, they are well aware of what they are doing, and they have a complete comprehension of the wider picture.

One of the characteristics of people who are good at persuasion is that they have a good understanding of the people they are attempting to influence, including what drives them and how far they are willing to go to achieve their goals. In this scenario, the person trying to convince you doesn't give morals any thought since doing so won't gain them what they want. They won't stop until they obtain what they want, and they'll use whatever methods necessary to get it.

For many years, the use of subliminal messaging has been referred to as the "dark art of persuasion." People have a tendency to link subliminal messaging with conspiracies against governments or advertising, and they assert that the messages are designed to control our thoughts and either lessen or alter our activities. No matter how hard we try, we will never be able to bring this kind of stimulation into our conscious awareness via the use of subliminal messaging, which is one of the most significant aspects of these types of communications. The second thing that we need to know is that individuals who believe in subliminal messages believe that it is a true consequence of communication that has been purposely created to produce a reaction from people and encourage them to do things that they usually wouldn't do. Those who don't believe in subliminal messaging don't believe that it is a real result of communication because they don't think it can be.

On the level of the subconscious, all of this takes place. However, we must differentiate between the subliminal and the supraliminal levels of perception. The difference between supraliminal and subliminal lies in the fact that supraliminal stimuli, despite their ability to elicit reactions and, as a result, impact our behaviors, are still perceptible to our conscious minds.

Freud is credited with coining the term "subconscious," which describes the portion of our minds that operates at a level of conscious awareness that is below the surface. "Our conscious mind provides us executive control of our thoughts. It is a private area where we conceal our wants, goals, and prior experiences that we no longer share with our conscious mind. We are able to think, assess, feel, and experience all of these things with awareness thanks to our consciousness. When it comes to our subconscious, this is not the case.

When it comes to the processing of information, our subconscious is constantly operating on autopilot and is far more powerful than our ordinary awareness. This might be risky because if someone is trying to influence how you think or behave by sending you subliminal signals, you won't be aware of what's going on, which can be unsettling.

Using NLP In Your Everyday Life And Relationships

In this book, I have made an effort to not only explain NLP to those who are unfamiliar with the area but also to elucidate its essence for those who have had past experience and training in the subject. It's not that difficult to do this at all, especially when you take into account how straightforward and tasteful the NLP Communication Model is. It can all be summed up in a single straightforward idea. Your filters have an effect on the images you have of yourself internally, as well as on your state and behavior. Because your filters determine how you interpret the world around you, altering them may cause significant changes in your experience of the world. That cannot be explained any more simply than that.

So, tell me, what exactly is the truth? This is not an issue that is normally addressed by writers of NLP books. On the other hand, there is a term that comes to mind that is often spoken by Matthew James, PhD, who is the president of American Pacific University. He said that regardless of what or who you believe yourself to be, the truth is that you are far more than that.

Although I do not consider Matt James to be a quantum physicist, the remark he made is consistent with the quantum thesis that the cosmos is full of an infinite number of possibilities and potentials, which are influenced by the limiting filters that we apply to it. When I read this, my mind instantly went to the many filters that are part of the NLP Communication Model. To tell you the truth, I don't really notice much of a difference. Our perception of reality is shaped by several filters. On the other hand, the reality that emerges as a consequence is more of a convenient illusion. Because of this, our present perception of reality is just a choice, and this has implications for not only our mental and emotional well-being, but also our physical health and our capacity for self-actualization. This is an option that comes with the responsibility of making a decision. If you are unhappy with your current reality, then using NLP methods may provide you with a sophisticated approach to discovering a new one.

Realizing that we function on several levels, as Robert Dilts said numerous times in his writings, is the source of a significant portion of our joy and, as a result, the key that unlocks the door to these boundless realities. Environment, habits, capabilities/strategies, beliefs and values, identity/mission, and spirituality/purpose are the components that make up these aspects. For the sake of this discussion, let us assume that the NLP Communication Model is present at each and every one of these levels. Every one of them has their very own one-of-a-kind filters, which leads to a distinct collection of internal representations and states.

The challenge that Dilts brings to our attention is the need that there be congruence between these several levels. For example, does your present conduct align with who you are as a person and/or the goals and aspirations you have for your life? If this is not the case, you will have a sense of discomfort. Even if I am simplifying Dilt's idea too much, I hope you get what I'm trying to say. Our filters have an impact on our moods as well as our behavior, but they do so on numerous levels all at once. Realizing the many different roles that you perform is yet another perspective on this topic that may be taken. For example, in addition to being a parent, a spouse, and a cognitive scientist, I also practice hypnotherapy. The issue that has to be answered is whether or not I am consistent in each of these roles. If this is not the case, then there is a need for change.

If you want to determine whether or not you have the potential to use NLP in your life, the first thing you need to do is determine whether or not you are experiencing a sense of dissonance. If this is the case, it would be suitable for you to perform some self-discovery as you investigate or calibrate your own condition, internal representations, and most importantly, your filters. You need to have an understanding of your meta-programs, beliefs, and values. If you are living a happy and peaceful existence, it is quite unlikely that you would feel the need or want to make any changes. To put it another way, you shouldn't mess with people's joy. On the other hand, if you have a persistent sensation of mental or physical pain, then you may choose to follow a deliberate program for change. This is especially the case if the discomfort is becoming worse. In such situation, the following is a list of questions that you should consider asking yourself:

1) What do I even am? Which am I, a "noun" or a "verb?" Am I a work of art that is always undergoing change or a person whose life is governed by predetermined rules and routines? Remember what Matt James said, that you are capable of far more than you give yourself credit for. By the way, if you want to change, it is usually helpful to think of yourself as a verb rather than a noun in your own life.

2) What are my core convictions? Where did they get there in the first place? Are they taught and conditioned in a certain way? Or, did I decide on them after conducting some kind of logical investigation? Do my beliefs hold me

hostage, or do I have the freedom to alter them whenever I please?

3) In my life, do I constantly respond to the circumstances that arise, or do I always try to create opportunities for myself and the people who are important to me?

4) Am I mainly driven by a desire to protect myself from harm and anguish? Or, am I driven by the want to do what I set out to do?

5) Do I feel that I am usually talking about "me" and otherwise always striving to validate myself by reminding the people around me of the things that I have accomplished and the views that I hold? Or do I spend my time worrying about how other people are feeling and about how they see me? (It is important to note that we are not equating this with the unhealthy role of a co-dependent at any point.)

6) Can I readily and effectively interact with other people? If this is the case, do they see an improvement after they are in my company?

Your responses to these questions might reveal a lot about your present situation and how you feel about it. They could also provide you with useful information on the chances you have to change. If you can never seem to get along with other people, you should work on strengthening your ability to form rapport. Becoming a better listener and demonstrating a genuine interest in other people is something you should work on if you have a habit of always insisting on being the "life of the party" and always bragging about your achievements and thoughts. If you do this, you will quickly realize how this may improve your life.

NLP approaches that are used by the individual themselves may also be of great assistance. Create a list of all the moments in your life when you were successful and resourceful and put them in order from most recent to least recent. You should then go backwards through your timeline to that moment and attach that resource. Next, travel ahead along your timeline to a future obstacle, cast off your anchor, and watch as your concerns melt away in an effortless and speedy manner. Figure out how to deprogram the unproductive and bad emotions you have and continually activate the positive resources you have. The field of neuro-linguistic programming (NLP) encompasses a broad variety of skills that are intended to alter your filters in such a way that your internal representations and emotional state enable you to build a version of yourself that is more desired.

Because of the manner that I have described NLP, I hope that you can now understand that despite the common misconception that it is a complex collection of procedures, it is really a pretty sophisticated and surprisingly straightforward idea that has a great deal of power. Simply altering your perspective will result in a different reality. Even if you just remember that one item after reading this book, you will have been incredibly successful. If you are motivated to further your NLP education, I wish you the best of luck in your endeavors.

What Are Some Of The Benefits And Drawbacks Of Manipulation?

The Advantages That Come With Employing Manipulation

The manner in which manipulation is used may have a significant impact on the kinds of outcomes that result from the process, and the range of those outcomes is directly proportional to the types of situations in which it can be applied. Even while we often consider manipulation to be a negative trait, there are really quite a few positive outcomes that may result from engaging in manipulative behavior in order to achieve our goals.

It is not always true that we will always bring damage to another person just because we are successful in obtaining what we desire. This is the key distinction between standard manipulation and the phenomenon that is referred to as "dark manipulation." It is necessary for us to differentiate between the two in this regard. When we engage in routine manipulation, our goal is to get something, but we don't want the other person to suffer any kind of injury or suffering in the process, whether it be on a mental, emotional, or physical level.

When it comes to dark manipulation, on the other hand, it is not going to make a difference to the manipulator whether or not the other person suffers any kind of pain. They do not care how severely that someone is injured, and it is expected that there will be some form of injury as a result of their actions. As long as the manipulator achieves the goal that they have set for themselves, they will be satisfied regardless of the circumstances.

Having said that, whether you are using manipulation to advance your agenda while benefiting others (for example, in sales or to gain some assistance on a collaborative project), or if you are using it to profit yourself, it is important to recognize that both scenarios include the use of manipulation. You don't care if someone is hurt in the process since you know that there are going to be some rewards that come with routinely engaging in manipulative behavior. You should look forward to receiving the following advantages, among others:

The use of manipulation is often going to be successful. If I know what I want and I know how to inspire a feeling in the other person so that they are more likely to do what I want, then manipulation will be successful, and we can evaluate this impact as well. The notion here is that if I know what I want and if I know how to evoke a feeling in the other person so that they are more likely to do what I want, then manipulation will be effective. Consider how everything fits together. Because companies are willing to invest billions of dollars in research and a variety of marketing methods in order to demonstrate how well the manipulation found in their campaigns and commercials works, we may deduce that manipulation is something that is successful.

Obviously, you need to carry out the tasks in the appropriate manner. It is not sufficient to just place an advertisement for a product on the internet or on television and anticipate a large number of customers as a result. Because there is simply too much competition out there, and because we often come into contact with so many commercials, it is hard for us to merely see something and then be misled by it. There has to be another level, and you need some experience and knowledge to pull it off, and that is what many different firms are investing their research resources in.

When we consider the typical forms of manipulation that a person will engage in, we may arrive to the same conclusion. It is not sufficient for us to just go up to another person and say, "Do what I want!" It is quite probable that the target will glance at us, chuckle, and then go without further interaction. You would behave in the same manner as well, wouldn't you? You have to make sure that you are using the appropriate strategies and that you have a good understanding of how the other person will react to what you say. You will discover to your delight, as a cool advantage, that manipulation is effective when it is used in the appropriate way and with the appropriate tactics.

The thought that we can become very skilled at manipulating others is the next advantage that comes along with the concept that manipulation is advantageous. You probably recognized at least a few instances in the past when you utilized manipulation to help you obtain what you wanted, even if the answers ended up surprise you while you were in the process of achieving your goal. Since long before we were even ready to take our first steps, we have been honing our skills in the art of manipulation.

This is due to the fact that there was a period of time when we were unable to communicate with one another yet we still needed to obtain goods. We needed to be fed and given something to drink in order to feel loved, to wear clothing, to have showers, to have our diapers changed, and other things. We were able to manipulate our parents into doing the job for us even though we were unable to communicate and express our ideas on our own and we were unable to take care of these things on our own at this time. Despite these limitations, we were still able to use manipulation to get our parents to do the work for us.

Because we have been able to read others from a young age to help us obtain what we wanted as a baby up through adulthood, we are already skilled at reading others, sometimes much better than we would expect, due to the fact that we have been able to read others from a young age to help us get what we wanted as a baby up through maturity. In addition, we may discover that, with a little bit of experience, we are able to rapidly estimate the appropriate action to do in order to assist us in motivating the other person involved in the process. Even while there are going to be those of us who are going to be much better at doing this than others, it is still something that we can work on to become better at and get some wonderful results with when it comes to influencing other people.

It is less difficult to get what we want. Imagine that you made the decision to approach the other person directly and ask them to grant your request in its entirety. If you ask them then, you may expect to get a negative response. Let's say you simply inquire about it without utilizing any of the tactics that we are going to go through in this handbook or any of the manipulative approaches that are out there. In such scenario, the other person does not have any obligation to assist you and will not have any feelings of guilt for engaging in activities in which they have no interest in participating.

However, if you are able to make use of some of the tools and tactics of manipulation that we have been talking about up to this point, and if you are able to provoke certain sentiments in the other person, you will find that it is much simpler to persuade the other person to do what you want them to. They are going to feel obligated to assist you in some way, even if they do not understand what it is that they are obligated to do. And even if the prospect of lending a hand with it is not something that appeals to them, there is a greater chance that they will agree to do so.

You are in for some really good news as a result of this. It means that you are going to be able to persuade the other person to say yes to what you want them to, without having to push them too hard or worry as much about whether they are going to say yes or no to you. It also means that you are going to be able to do this without having to worry about whether they are going to say yes or no to you. You will have already put in the effort that is necessary to persuade them to work with you, and it is probable, particularly if you spent time evaluating them and utilizing the correct strategy for their requirements, that they are going to agree to what it is that you want to accomplish.

And last, the concept of power is going to be the subject of our discussion here with regard to the advantages that may be gained via the use of manipulation and the many strategies that are associated with it. owing to the fact that there is certain to be an element of power present in all relationships, whether they familial, professional, or otherwise, including romantic connections. Manipulation is going to be the weapon that we need to make sure that we obtain that power over our target, which is something that all of us would want to have control over other people, or at least over someone at some time in our lives.

Now, some people will abuse the authority they have and push it to an extreme. This is the point at which the manipulation is going to morph into abuse, in addition to causing a few additional difficulties. But the power that comes with manipulation can sometimes be as simple as having a little of control over one person in your life, even your kid, and it doesn't always have to be an abusive or terrible type of thing to deal with. Sometimes it's just having a bit of influence over one person in your life.

The sixth day features ABC-NLP, a fusion of NLP and behavioral science.

The following is our well guarded method for demonstrating the genuineness of the NLP in an objective manner. In order to better complement NLP, we adopted this strategy from the field of Organizational Behavior Management (OBM). OBM refers to a style of behaviour in which employees of firms and corporations are subjected to some kind of operational conditioning. Why did they bother to use science to establish that the OBM was effective? Experiments using a single-blind randomization could not be carried out since doing so would require creating two identical duplicates of a business. What they have been able to do instead is (a) demonstrate that they operate on the concepts of the Experimental Behavior Analysis, which is a scientific method for the analysis of behavior in a laboratory that has a strong scientific base with a significant amount of research that has been peer-reviewed and published in scientific journals, and (b) prove that their tests show a significant and positive change after their involvement in a company. These two accomplishments are what they have been able to do. Both of these factors provide OBM the scientific evidence that it requires.

The same goes for the Neuro-Linguistic Programming (NLP). Because NLP is a tool for modeling human behaviors, it is fairly simple to create the strategies of BehavioralBehavior Analysis and utilize those approaches to guide the research that we perform inside NLP. This is because NLP is a tool for modeling human behaviors. In point of fact, the fact that we have done this has brought us to the Behavior Analysis System used by ABC. It was discovered that the brain is capable of three primary modes of thought, which are as follows:

impression, associative learning, and instrumental learning.

Because the impression doesn't appear until after the conception, its appeal is quite restricted as a result. Associative thinking would be impossible without the use of NLP. The brain engages in a process known as associative thinking when it creates a probabilistic relationship between two different sensory events. For instance, when your brain sees smoke, it immediately assumes there is a fire. Not only do we use anchoring as a method for developing constructive linkages, but also... However, we also utilize NLP to dismantle negative connections and build more positive associations with almost every NLP practice that we do.

Instrumental learning is the third kind of information acquisition that takes place in our brains; nevertheless, the NLP does not take this into account. Through a process known as instrumental learning, our brains are able to construct a probabilistic connection between our actions and the probability of a variety of events. The most apparent illustration of this is the method in which we open doors. Our subconscious has learned that this particular action is the most effective way to get us what we desire, which in this case is space to pass through a curtain.

The finest description of how instrumental learning takes place may be found in the ABC model. Conduct is represented by the letter B in the ABC paradigm. A stands for antecedents, which include everything that takes place before someone acts or the items that a person must have in order to be able to behave in a certain manner. Nearly everyone, including the vast majority of those working in the area of NLP, engages in historical contemplation. They instruct others on how to conduct themselves, teach and coach others, and so on. All of this is going to take place before a specific person responds in a certain way.

The letter C in the ABC model denotes the concept of "Consequences," which includes everything that takes place as a result of a person's actions in a particular way. Virtually no one pays a great deal of attention to what occurs after this. Despite this, the data unequivocally demonstrates that the events that have place after that have a far greater impact on subsequent conduct than the occurrences that take place after that. In other words, the effect of the Consequences is far more significant than the influence of the Precedents in this scenario.

The fact that the ABC model may be used over a period of time is one of its most attractive features. First there are the Actions, then there are the Ancestors, and last there are the Consequences. Additionally, it is a probabilistic paradigm in and of itself. Only the relationships that make such acts more or less possible are shown by this information. The ABC model, like the NLP, takes a firm stance against claims that link causes and effects, although the ABC model may still be considered scientific. After stating at the beginning of this section that we would look for areas of science in which claims of cause and effect are not applicable, we have finally located such areas! In the case of triangulation, the empirical Bayesian equations and the ABC model both operate independently of cause and effect, despite the fact that they are both philosophically and logically sound.

On top of that, we should extend the use of conventional NLP methods such as accelerated phobia cure and timeline research to break down negative patterns based on instrumental learning and replace them with constructive patterns in the same manner that NLP already does with negative patterns based on associative thinking. This would be similar to the way that NLP breaks down negative patterns based on associative thinking and replaces them with constructive patterns. All of this is taught to you beginning on day six.

Techniques Often Used In Nlp

The methods of NLP are quite effective. The outcomes are stunning and remarkable, yet the procedure that led to them is quite straightforward, easy to grasp, and straightforward to put into practice in your day-to-day life. The following are some of the strategies that NLP coaches and trainers utilize to assist their clients in making positive changes in their lives.

Questioning of the Meta Model

The most successful NLP coaches are aware of and comprehend the significance of asking the appropriate questions in order to generate replies from their subjects that have the potential to alter their points of view. If you ask the proper questions to anybody, including yourself, you will be able to acquire answers that shed fresh light on the way the world seems to you. In reality, this is true. If you ask the correct questions to anyone, including yourself, you will get these answers.

The NLP Meta Model is based on a collection of linguistic approaches that center on the elimination, modification, and generalization of words and expressions that are common in everyday conversation. Many of our issues have their origins in the conscious use of language that we employ on a daily basis, and this is particularly true when we are having dialogues with ourselves. The Meta Model requires us to ask the enlightening questions that drag us out of our sleep and point us in the direction of potential answers to the issues we face.

A line of inquiry based on the Meta Model helps us become more aware of a fundamental reality, which is the realization that we are already familiar with both the primary challenge and the answer to it. But since we do not desire the solution that is proposed to us, we avoid the issue altogether in the vain hope that we will eventually come across one that is more suited to our needs. Here is an illustration of that:

Jo: Some of the time, my girlfriend can be rather irritating.

The most basic reaction would be why, and what exactly is she doing to irritate you?

This reaction, possibly inadvertently, focuses on the precise activities taken by Jo's girlfriend that irritate her. Let's have a look at the same scenario with a response based on a Meta Model, shall we?

Jo: Some of the time, my girlfriend can be rather irritating.

What specific occurrence irritates you the most and why do you find it so difficult to deal with?

By reorienting the questions in relation to the topic at hand, the NLP model enables individuals to get a fresh perspective on familiar predicaments.

The Approach Through Modeling

This strategy is for those who are aware of the outcomes they want but are unsure how to go about achieving those outcomes. Creating a route for oneself requires a significant investment of time, energy, and effort. The modeling strategy will be helpful here because of the situation. There is someone out there who has already put in the time and effort to practice and perfect the ability or the information that you are looking to acquire, regardless of where you want to end up.

The fundamental concept behind the NLP modeling strategy is to model yourself after someone else who excels in the same area in which you are now struggling. This strategy teaches you not to squander resources by attempting to create something entirely new. The only thing you need to do is choose the ideal role model, then carefully replicate that person's actions while making any necessary adjustments to make them work for you. Therefore, if you want to become an NLP coach, you should look for someone to model yourself after and then do what they do.

The Method of the New Behavior Generator (NBG)

You need to keep in mind that you are the director of your own life, as well as the actor in it, in order to do this. Therefore, the director in you has to convince the actor to engage in other behaviors and come up with new behaviors that will assist you in accomplishing what it is that you want to do. Imagine what it is that you want to accomplish, and then engage in actions that will turn that image that you have in your mind into a reality in the actual world.

Using a Method Called Re-imprinting

Throughout your life, I have no doubt that you have found yourself in situations when you were feeling confident and ready to take on the world, only to be overcome by unexplainable anxiety and panic attacks. These are the nervous times that happen often, and when they do, you start to question yourself about things like, "What went wrong?"

This might have been triggered by a previous unsuccessful experience or any other imprints in our thoughts, and trust me when I say that everyone of us has enough of imprints firmly entrenched inside our psyche. The re-imprinting approach requires you to reimagine or reinterpret your past experiences in such a manner that there are large positive impacts rather than anxieties and nervous sensations as a result of using this technique.

The Technique for Changing One's Limiting Beliefs

Experiences that leave a mess in our brains and wreak havoc on our development are one factor that stands in the way of our progress. Further, profoundly conditioned restricted beliefs provide yet another category of obstacles to personal development. These are either conditioned by our upbringing or by certain events and/or experiences of the past that have produced these boundaries, and we are terrified to breach these barriers because of them. These constraints have caused us to feel limited, and we are conditioned to feel limited. These restricting ideas cause you to miss out on possibilities that are already available, thus it is essential that you either dismantle these beliefs or, at the very least, reinterpret them.

Utilizing a Method Called Memory Dissociation

When you make an effort to alter your way of life, you will always awaken painful memories that, until now, have been dormant like the proverbial dogs with their tails between their legs. Now, in the event that you decide to rouse these dozing canines, you will be required to revisit these embarrassing recollections. It is essential to relive them so that they may be eliminated from your system as quickly as possible. However, it needs to be done without living 'in' them again. This approach teaches you to look at painful memories from the outside, get wisdom from them, and then let go of those memories when you have done so.

Workouts That Focus On Building Muscle

1. Creating models. Find someone who has been successful in the field in which you want to be successful as well and model your behavior after them. What kinds of actions and characteristics does this individual typically engage in? Which choice did she make that allowed her to have such success? What are some of their routines? You should make an effort to write it down on a piece of paper, and then, using your notes as a guide, you should try to incorporate these concepts into your regular life step by step.

2. The practice of anchoring. Unwind and make yourself at home. Determine the feeling that you wish to serve as your point of reference; for example, make it preparedness to take action. Think back

to a time in the past when you felt the same way and recall the circumstances. In order to strengthen this impression, it amplifies the visual, aural, and kinesthetic inputs (picture, word, action). The anchor has to be placed in the state of having the most intense feelings possible, which is being ready to act. Perform this task a number of times so that the order of events will become ingrained in your memory.

3. An example of a metaphor. While you are having a conversation with your interlocutor, you should make an effort to identify the metaphors he uses and then interpret them literally. You should make an effort to evaluate it literally in order to get to the heart of the matter and find a solution to the difficulty that your interlocutor is having.

4. A chronology. Consider the speed at which time moves while you are having

fun. While you are working. When you are now awaiting the arrival of something. You may look at it by dispersing these occurrences throughout the line of time, which will make you feel more comfortable participating in things that you like less. Incorporate some sub-modalities into this.

5. To reframe Do you enjoy it when it rains? Consider how you would react emotionally if you were caught in the rain without an umbrella on you. In what setting would anything like this be considered a positive? Look for the good that can come from the incident that happened this week, and give some thought to the more profound implications of what it may bring you if you approach it in a positive light. Consider the difference between rain and a dry, arid landscape. Make a change in your circumstances as well, so that

you may start looking for the beneficial consequences that this incident has had on you, even if at first sight it may not seem that this is the case.

Swish Pattern is number six. Choose the practice or pattern of behavior that you wish to alter. Examine what leads to undesirable conduct, what the stimuli is that prompts you to visualize it in all its gory detail, and so on. Let it be a vivid vision much like the ones you saw in the visualizations. Consider what alternative behavior you would want to see adopted in lieu of the undesirable one that you perceive from the vantage point of the observer. Reduce the brightness and volume of the picture on the left that you do not want to view, then boost the volume of the image on the right that you do want to see so that you can see both at the same time. They instantly magnify the positive picture while simultaneously decreasing the size of the negative image. After each session, you should open your eyes and carry out the activity once again. Repeat it multiple times until the mental picture that is linked with the undesirable habit is automatically replaced with the occurrence that you wish to take its place.

7. Mental pictures. Put your feet up, shut your eyes, and concentrate on taking slow, even breaths. Imagine a setting from the future in which the sensations of sight, hearing, and touch are amplified to a far greater degree. Imagine and prepare yourself for the good feelings that will come with achieving your objective. Increase the size of this picture as much as you can. Let there be an even greater variety of colors. You should go through this process as many times as necessary in order to properly orient yourself in order to achieve your objective.

www.ingramcontent.com/pod-product-compliance
Lightning Source LLC
Chambersburg PA
CBHW052134110526
44591CB00012B/1713